How Internet Radio Can
Change the World

How Internet Radio Can Change the World

✦

An Activist's Handbook

Eric Lee

iUniverse, Inc.
New York Lincoln Shanghai

How Internet Radio Can Change the World
An Activist's Handbook

iUniverse books may be ordered through booksellers or by contacting:

iUniverse
2021 Pine Lake Road, Suite 100
Lincoln, NE 68512
www.iuniverse.com
1-800-Authors (1-800-288-4677)

ISBN: 0-595-34965-X

Printed in the United States of America

Contents

Introduction

Trade unions and progressive organizations should use every technology that comes their way—if that technology can improve communications and strengthen their organizations.

After all, this is what the opposition does (the opposition being giant multinational corporations and their allies). Every new communications technology is first adopted by those institutions with the means to purchase and use it. Because new technologies tend to be expensive at first, wealthy corporations and governments are invariably the first adopters.

What this means in practice is that each technological shift—from telexes to fax machines to email, from land line phones to mobiles, from print newsletters to websites—is first adopted by those in power. Later—often much later—grassroots organizations like trade unions, environmental groups and human rights organizations slowly take up the new technology, particularly as it grows cheaper. There is nearly always a gap, sometimes of many years, between the adoption of new technology first by ruling elites and later by popular movements.

I am most familiar with the trade union movement and many of the examples in this book will come from that experience. For the last decade or so, I have been involved in an effort to persuade unions all over the world to adopt some of the new communications technologies (in particular, email and the web)—and to use them intelligently.

It has been a long and difficult effort and we are not even close to completion, but at least now nearly all the major unions of the world, in both developed and developing countries, now use the web and email. The same has long been true of other progressive organizations. Indeed environmental, human rights and women's organizations were often far ahead of the unions in their adoption of the new technology.

You can make a strong case for using such tools as email and the web on the grounds of cost and increased productivity. After all, it's a lot cheaper and faster to send out a newsletter by email than it is to print and post through the mail. It's probably not surprising that one of my early allies in the efforts to bring unions online was the Treasurer of a large trade union.

Using these new technologies often does save money. But it was not for reasons of cost and efficiency that I have become so enthusiastic about the Internet.

I'm excited because the Internet allows unions and other progressive organizations to rediscover an idea that we had long thought to be dead and buried: the idea of internationalism.

INTERNATIONALISM

A hundred years ago, when a pre-World War I version of "globalization" was in full bloom, the trade unions and socialist parties of the world were living through a kind of golden age of internationalism. As early as 1864, when Karl Marx and conservative British trade union officials formed the organization that became known as the International Workingmen's Association (or more commonly, the First International), they understood the importance of internationalism. When you joined the First International, you received a membership card from its central office in London. You understood from that moment that you belonged to a global movement.

That understanding persisted for decades. The First International lasted only a few years, but the organization that replaced it in 1889 (known as the Second International) has persisted in various forms until today. And during those years up until 1914, internationalism was a part of the way people thought—people in the trade union and socialist movements.

When workers in one country would go on strike, workers in neighboring countries would contribute money—as much as a full day's wages—to solidarity funds. Union organizers traveled from country to country easily (this was in the years when passports were not needed to cross national borders). Unions often had members in a number of countries, and this was particularly true in the English speaking world. British unions had Australian affiliates, in North America unions had members on both sides of the US/Canadian border, and some of the largest unions in Ireland were part and parcel of the British trade union movement.

By the 1890s, global organizations of workers in specific industries were being formed, among them the International Metalworkers Federation and the International Transport Workers Federation. These bodies became known as international trade secretariats and they persist to this day—but they are now called global union federations.

In the early years of the twentieth century, globalization as we know it was not yet in full bloom, but workers' organizations were acting as if it was. Faced with the challenge of a world war just over the horizon, the unions and their political parties agreed that the war could be stopped—and would be stopped—by the collective organization of workers in all the warring countries. After all, a highlight of international socialist congresses was an event like the famous handshake between leading Japanese and Russian socialists—while their countries were at war.

By 1914, it was widely assumed that the outbreak of war between France and Germany would result in a general strike in both countries. At least that's what the unions and their socialist and labor parties had agreed to. But when the First World War broke out in August of that year, the unions and the majority of their political representatives swung behind their national governments.

The international organizations of socialist parties and trade unions collapsed, and with them the dream of a world without borders and without wars.

There were of course attempts to revive the International during that war and in its aftermath, but the labor movement was soon divided into two hostile camps—the supporters of Lenin and the Bolsheviks, and their opponents. As if that wasn't a serious enough blow, the rise of fascism in Italy and Germany, and then Stalinism in the USSR, dealt crushing defeats to the international labor movement.

Following the Second World War, there was once again hope that internationalism could be revived, but this was soon dashed by the experience of the Cold War. Unions and their political parties quickly lined up on one side or another of that global conflict. There were shameful episodes of unions in the West collaborating with intelligence agencies like the CIA. Meanwhile, Communist unions and parties happily cooperated with Stalinist regimes that persecuted and killed oppositionists.

I know I've gone on a bit about some history that is probably not very familiar to many of you, but I want to put the rise of the Internet in a kind of context. And that context is a paradox.

When the world economy was not yet fully globalized, unions and their allies behaved as if there were no borders and were able to wage concerted global campaigns for things like the eight-hour day. At the first congress of the Second International, held in Paris in 1889, it was decided to hold a worldwide day of demonstrations and protests to demand an eight-hour working day. The date set was 1 May 1890, and workers all around the world did indeed rally and march in support of a commonly-agreed goal. That day—May Day—has been celebrated ever since as the international workers' holiday.

Today, living in a completely globalized world, capitalists behave like there are no borders, and trade unionists put bumper stickers of their country's flag on their cars, with slogans like "Buy American" or "Buy British".

Unions are barely involved any more in international solidarity work, and the international organizations they created—the global union federations and the International Confederation of Free Trade Unions (ICFTU)—are under-staffed, under-funded and largely incapable of meeting the challenges of a twenty-first century global economy.

By the early 1990s, the situation seemed rather grim indeed. The giant transnational corporations seemed to have won. There was a growing intellectual consensus promoted by the World Bank and International Monetary Fund. It argued that neo-liberal economic policies such as those promoted by Margaret Thatcher and Ronald Reagan needed to be adopted by all countries, in both the developed and developing worlds. Corporations controlled vast media empires, with television, radio, newspapers, magazines, and book publishing increasingly concentrated in the hands of only a few.

Unions were everywhere in decline, socialism was a dirty word on both sides of the now-fallen Iron Curtain, and in the views of some Western intellectuals, history was over.

And then at that moment, something remarkable happened.

The World Wide Web was born. Suddenly trade unions, environmental groups, women's organizations, the human rights movement—everyone—had websites. The playing field was being leveled. The same means of communication which had once been so expensive that few could afford them had become cheap. An international newsletter, which could once only be published by the very richest of organizations, could now be done free of charge. Overnight, things changed.

By the turn of the century, grassroots activists were using the Internet in countless ways to challenge the new world order. Unions were waging global campaigns in support of workers rights and against neo-liberal economic policies. Environmental groups, always more skillful than unions in using the new communications technologies, were taking them to higher levels. For activists in groups like Amnesty International, adding on the technology of the Internet to traditional campaigning had the effect of attaching a jet engine to a Vespa. The explosion of anti-globalization protests, starting in Seattle in 1999, was coordinated online.

Global campaigning was becoming real, and a new internationalism was being born.

And yet the reluctance to try new technologies is still there. There are many reasons why this is so, including the relatively high cost of most new technologies. Which is why the corporations try them first. To this day, you are far more likely to encounter a technology like videoconferencing in a corporate headquarters than in a union one.

At this point, you're probably already thinking—hey, I thought this was a book about Internet radio? And so far I've been talking to you about Karl Marx and May Day and neo-liberalism. Where's the radio stuff?

I do appreciate your patience, really. But I want to emphasize that what we're talking about here, in this book, is *social change*. What we all want to do is make the world a better place. Getting rid of child labor, abolishing the death penalty, stopping global warming, ending Third World poverty, eliminating all forms of racial and sexual discrimination—these are all things that people in progressive organizations, including unions, want. And they want them all over the world—the very same things.

To change the world, we have to communicate much better than we do now. Which is why I support trying out every new means of communication as it comes our way.

The fax machine was a huge advance over the telex. Among other things, you had to be a trained operator to use a telex. Email was a huge advance over fax machines. The web is a far superior way to publish news and information as compared to traditional print newsletters, especially for global communications.

And there are more cutting edge applications that trade unionists and other progressives should be exploring now. Among these is Voice over Internet Protocol (VoIP), a way of using your computer as a telephone. Why would you want to do that, you might ask? After all, isn't it simpler to use the phone right here on my desk? Yes, it is. But what if you're in San Francisco and you want to call Lagos. Or, even more important, what if it's the opposite—you're in Lagos and want to call overseas. VoIP is so cheap, that for many of us, it has turned what were previously prohibitively expensive international telephone calls into something which is completely free of charge.

These technologies are transforming the way we communicate. And by making our communications global, they are opening new possibilities to change an ever-more-global world.

RADIO AND INTERNET RADIO

Which brings us to the beginning: Internet radio. That's what the rest of this book is going to be about.

Before jumping to Internet radio itself—indeed, even before defining the term—I want to spend a moment on its predecessor, radio.

There is a bit of controversy surrounding who "invented" radio. Apparently, by 1873, the theoretical possibility of radio was first proposed by James Clerk Maxwell, the eminent Scottish physicist. Five years later, David E. Hughes, a music professor in Kentucky, transmitted and received radio waves, but no one noticed this. It wasn't until 1893—twenty years after Maxwell first proposed the possibility of radio—that the controversial Serbian-American inventor Nikola Tesla first demonstrated radio communications.

You would think then that Tesla is the father of radio, but an Italian engineer named Guglielmo Marconi got a lot of the credit. This is because three years after Tesla, Marconi got himself a patent as the inventor of wireless telegraphy and a year later set up the world's first radio station on the Isle of Wight, in England. Historians continue to dispute who actually "invented" radio, with Marconi and Tesla in close competition.

What is not in dispute is the incredibly rapid rise of radio once Marconi began to develop it. The explosion of interest in radio very closely parallels the rise of the Internet decades later.

In the US, for example, the first commercial radio broadcast took place in November, 1920. Only 13 years later, nearly two-thirds of households in the US had radio stations. That was a real revolution in communications.

The 1930s was a time when radio was extensively used for political purposes in the United States. President Franklin D. Roosevelt had huge success with his "fireside chats". The reactionary priest Father Coughlin used the same medium to promote anti-Semitic and pro-Nazi policies. The thing to remember is that radio was a brand-new medium, and that only a few years earlier, no one owned a radio and few could imagine what it would be used for.

The early days of radio also saw Utopian visions for its use which paralleled those later claimed for the Internet. The American Utopian socialist author Edward Bellamy featured a vision of radio in his novel, "Looking Backward". Even US President Herbert Hoover (hardly a radical) was over-the-top with his praise for this new-fangled invention. "For the first time in human history we have available to us the ability to communicate simultaneously with millions of our fellow men," he wrote. He expect that radio would furnish men with "entertainment, instruction, widening vision of national problems and national events."

But there was only one problem with radio as it developed in the 1920s and later: eventually, it required huge amounts of money, and government approval, to broadcast. After a few years, everyone had receivers in their homes, but very few could transmit, and only government-licensed radio stations could truly broadcast to large audiences.

Instead of being a force for human liberation, radio was increasingly used by authoritarian regimes and giant corporations to spread their own messages, whether that message was to whip up anti-Semitism or to sell soap.

One of the extraordinary things that happened with radio was its survival long after competing technologies emerged on the scene. Once there were sound movies, a decade after radio first became a mass medium, people found themselves going to the movies where they could see and hear newsreels and concerts and commercial films—but they also enjoyed listening to music and drama and news in the comfort of their homes. The emergence of television threatened to kill off radio again, but radio happily co-existed with the new medium and has done so for more than fifty years now.

One should pause and think about radio's survival. What is it about radio that makes it different from, say, television? Why would we want to continue to use this hundred-year old technology when there are new, improved versions around?

I think there are a few advantages to radio that it's important to keep in mind once we come around to Internet radio, and these include the following:

To absorb what radio has to offer you only need to use your ears. You can do other things while listening to radio. Many of us cook, clean, and drive with the radio on.

From the 1950s on, with the invention of portable transistor radios that ran on batteries, radio became a means of communication like no other. Using a radio, you could be in the middle of a field or on a beach with no other human being in sight, and yet be listening to the live broadcast of a human voice. Portable televisions never took off the way portable radios did.

Despite government control, despite the initially high set-up costs, radio remains a vastly more diverse means of communication than television. A quarter of a century ago, before leaving the US to live abroad, I was given a Sony shortwave radio as a going away present from a friend in Wisconsin. For years, it was a lifeline to the outside world, allowing me to discover the BBC World Service. Later I came to know countless other stations and could enjoy a range of music, news and features that were unavailable on local television and radio stations.

There are probably other advantages to radio as well as these. And these advantages are why radio continues to be so popular despite the various inventions that have followed it.

When we go into the subject of Internet radio in greater detail you'll see that it preserves and vastly expands some of radio's advantages. Internet radio offers far more diversity than even the most powerful shortwave set.

But Internet radio has not yet reproduced the portability of radio, meaning that you cannot take it to the beach, nor drive while listening to it.

But I get ahead of myself—first we need to explore together what Internet radio is, and where it comes from.

A Technology Designed by Activists, For Activists

This book is going to make the case that Internet Radio represents a powerful new tool which activists can use. But before going even one step forward, we need to take a step back and define what we mean by "Internet radio."

The simple definition would be something like this: *Internet radio is the continuous transmission of streaming audio over the Internet.*

We are speaking about a transmission of content; Internet radio is first and foremost a form of broadcasting. There must be a broadcaster sending out content, just as a radio station does. And there must be a way for listeners to listen in to this content.

That transmission must be continuous. It need not be 24/7 as indeed many "normal" radio stations do not broadcast all the time.

Internet radio refers to audio content. It is possible, and has been possible for nearly a decade now, to broadcast video as well, and we'll come to this later on. But Internet radio means audio—music, talk, animal sounds, whatever.

In defining what Internet radio is, we are already beginning to make clear what it isn't.

Internet radio is not the same thing as putting up some MP3 files on your website. It is not the same thing as sharing audio files with friends and strangers through peer-to-peer networks.

That having been said, there are at least three types of Internet radio stations.

11

First, there are those which exist in the non-Internet world, and which in addition to broadcasting via radio waves also broadcast the same content via the net. The BBC World Service fits in this category. Though most of its listeners still use the traditional radio broadcasts, an increasing percentage of its listenership comes through the net. Not long ago, the BBC decided—as a cost-saving move—to stop shortwave broadcasts to those parts of the world where Internet penetration meant listeners could hear their favorite programs online.

Second, there are Internet-only radio stations which do not broadcast via radio waves. Radio LabourStart, which I founded in 2004, is in this category. There will be a whole chapter about it later in this book.

And finally, there are those stations which violate my own definition of Internet radio and which offer up loads of content, but do not stream this continuously. Some would say that in so doing, they are exploiting an advantage offered by the web, but more on that later. Radio Nation, which we'll discuss in the next chapter, fits into this category.

The lines between these various types of Internet radio stations can get blurred a bit.

For example, an Internet-only radio station can have its content picked up and re-transmitted via radio. (This raises some interesting possibilities for activists, and particularly for those of us who wish to reach regions of the world where Internet access is rare, but transistor radios are common. More on this in the final chapter.)

Or a more conventional radio station might have Internet-specific content, not broadcast via radio waves.

In my definition of Internet radio, I made reference to "streaming audio" and this is an important concept.

Most of us by now have some vague sense of how the Internet works. We sort of understand that there are these things called web pages and that by clicking on links we are somehow sending out an instruction to retrieve these pages to our computer and display them on our screen.

More than a decade ago, at the dawn of the Internet, the same principle applied to audio files. If I wanted to share a song with visitors to my website, I could upload a digital version of the song, and you could click on a link and the song would begin to download to your computer. Once the song had completed its download and every last byte was on your hard drive—and only then—you could play the song, with the appropriate software.

To understand the revolutionary effect of the introduction of streaming audio, you have to remember that back then, in the mid-1990s, every home user of the Internet and many users at work were dialing up at speeds that now seem incredibly slow. The 14,400 kbps modem was then common.

The downloading of even a single song, particularly in non-compressed formats, could take a very, very long time. The downloading of an entire album—perhaps an entire day.

By the early 1990s, much music had already been digitized and compact disks were already quite common. But the downloading of digital music from the Internet was a painful process. The future of CD sales seemed secure.

But over the next several years, two innovations would change all that—the invention of *streaming* audio on the one hand and the roll-out of broadband Internet to millions of users on the other.

The solution to the problem of downloading audio files was the invention of streaming audio. Basically this meant the writing of software which began playing the song before the download was complete. It also meant that the song had to be in a highly compressed format—after all, what's the point of beginning to slowly play a 3 minute song that's going to take 45 minutes to download?

Streaming audio exploits the concept of *buffering*, and this is an important concept to understand. When you send out an instruction from your computer to download an audio file—and this can be a streamed file or it can just be an ordinary digital audio file sitting on some server—the server responds by sending you the file in *packets*. A single song will be broken up into a very large number of these packets. And the packets are routed to you through the Internet through many different servers. Every time a packet is sent, your computer has to confirm that it's been received, and the packets have to be re-assembled at your end for playing. Think of those machines on "Star Trek" that would beam you down to the planet, disassembling and then reassembling your molecules.

The solution to the problems of dealing with all those packets is to *buffer* them—which means that your computer waits a few seconds, makes sure it has enough packets to start playing the song, and then continuously collects more packets and checks them. Sometimes the playing of an audio file will stop because your computer doesn't have enough of those packets ready—and that's when you'll see a "buffering error" appear.

The slower your connection to the Internet, the more likely these errors are to happen. On a high-speed connection, you rarely get buffering problems these days.

ROB GLASER AND REALNETWORKS

The most popular of these early streaming audio players was called "RealAudio". It was extremely impressive, but because of the compression of large audio files into compact ones and the slowness of the average Internet connection, there was an inevitable degradation of sound quality. The worst portable transistor radio produced better quality sound. Nevertheless, RealAudio was a breakthrough. It paved the way for bigger and better things.

RealAudio was produced by a company called Progressive Networks that was founded in 1993 by Rob Glazer. As Business Week once put it, Progressive Networks was a "company that hoped to deliver socially conscious programming over the Web. The company's focus shifted when it became apparent that the streaming-media technology that it had pioneered could become a nifty business on its own." That sounds a little odd—did Glaser really create RealAudio as a way of changing the world, and only later on, learned from others that it might have other uses?

On the face of it, this sounds absurd. Progressive Networks (now known as Real-Networks) today employs over 700 people and has a market capitalization of just over a billion US dollars. But we are expected to believe that back in 1994, Rob Glaser was just thinking about delivering "socially conscious programming over the web."

Well, there is some evidence that this just might be the case. Business Week says that Glaser remains today "an unusual mix of capitalist and liberal do-gooder." A corporate official at RealNetworks says of Glaser that "his politics are usually to the left of Che Guevara."

Glaser's background gives us a clue of his real motives in launching RealAudio a decade ago. His parents were political activists. His father ran a small printing press in Yonkers, New York and his mother was a social worker, working with at-risk children in inner city New York. When Glaser was twelve, he handed out leaflets against the nuclear arms race, and supported the United Farm Workers, who were at that time urging consumers to boycott grapes. Glaser's parents sent him to a special school offering a humanistic education.

In 1979, when Glaser attended Yale University, he was already something of a left-wing activist. Renewed Cold War tensions were causing the US government to revive certain elements of the Selective Service System in preparation for a possible renewal of conscription. Glaser refused to register and participated in demonstrations against the draft and for disarmament. He ran an organization called the "Campaign Against Militarism and the Draft." His column for The Yale Daily News—where he was editorial page editor—was called "What's Left". He supported workers on campus who were struggling to form a union.

Glaser was a political activist and computer geek at the same time, and reportedly considered working as an organizer for the farmworkers union. But by the 1980s he found himself working for Microsoft, where he rapidly rose in the ranks. But by the early 1990s, he lost an argument over control of the company's multimedia operations, prompting him to resign.

Together with one of his buddies from Yale, David Halperin, Glaser came up with a vague plan for a company that would link television to the Internet "in the service of progressive causes." The years at Microsoft apparently did little or nothing to dim his enthusiasm for political activism.

Later on, this was refined to focus on audio, and in particular on the new concept of "streaming media". According to his partner Halperin (who later became a Clinton speech writer), the new company would become "a place where people who wanted to change the world could go".

"It's fair to say that our original objective was social revolution," said Halperin later. As Wired magazine put it, "they wanted to democratize the media and be able to deliver their progressive message over the Internet, bypassing corporate media giants."

Glaser and Halperin decided to demonstrate a working model of streaming media to a "an informal group of liberal advisers" in a hotel in Washington, D.C. "We've developed a proprietary technology that I think will be critically important to our goals," Glaser reportedly said. He flipped on his laptop and played a streamed audio file of a baseball game. The "liberal advisers" immediately grasped something that Glaser hadn't: streaming multimedia didn't exist merely to change the world. You could make money from it too. Afterwards you could donate some of the profits to liberal causes, if you still wanted to.

Amazingly, it seems as if Glaser—who had just completed a decade or so working for Microsoft—had never thought of RealNetworks as a business. He actually seems to have been motivated by idealism.

I find it fascinating that before the first Internet radio stations were a twinkle in anyone's eye, the man who did more than anyone to make them a possibility had a plan to change the world.

As an official Glazer website puts it, "Voices that could not penetrate mainstream media could now be heard in real time worldwide over the Internet."

That was back in 1993 when the company was founded. By 1995 RealAudio was a reality, and two years later, RealVideo followed. The company renamed itself RealNetworks, but Glaser's website today still emphasizes that the software it creates "continues to deliver independent and alternative ideas along with a vast array of content".

In 1996, Glazer launched WebActive, a website designed to promote progressive websites, especially those that used streaming multimedia.

Meanwhile Glaser continues to donate huge sums to progressive causes. It was estimated that he gave over $1 million to the failed effort to defeat George Bush in 2004. His company has been called a political "incubator" because so many progressive politicians have worked for it, including Democratic Senator Maria Cantwell from Washington.

Glaser eventually set up a foundation, the Glaser Progress Foundation, which funds many of the innovative uses of streaming multimedia—including Internet radio—by progressive organizations. We will come across it again later in this book.

But his real contribution to social change may well turn out to be not so much his donations to progressive causes but the software itself. His original vision of a product that could change the world—even though dismissed by those "liberal advisers" in a Washington hotel a decade ago—may yet turn out to be true.

The success of RealAudio triggered a number of competitors, most prominently Microsoft's Windows Media Player. One presumes that Microsoft was *not* creating software to change the world, empower the poor, and so on. From the very beginning, Microsoft saw the possibility of making a profit with streaming media, as did Apple with its QuickTime product. To those companies, as indeed to RealNetworks, the technology was best used to stream the content produced by the giant media companies, which paid to use server software that could stream the content to ever-growing numbers of listeners on the net.

At the same time as streaming multimedia was becoming a big deal, the rise of the MP3 file format would itself make a huge contribution to the possibility of Internet radio.

JUSTIN FRANKEL AND NULLSOFT

MP3 is simply a file format, just like a Microsoft Word document is a file format, or a JPEG image is a file format. What made MP3 special was that it allowed the compression of digital music at a very high quality. This meant that even if you weren't streaming—if you just wanted to take the songs from the net and put them onto your computer and play them through your speakers—you could now do this. MP3 files are small files that sound like big files.

Many companies created software and then hardware to play such music (the most famous example of the latter being the Apple iPod). But one company stands out because of the role it played in the Internet radio revolution. That company was called Nullsoft and it was founded in 1997 by an 18-year named Justin Frankel.

Frankel wrote a program called Winamp which was designed to play MP3 music on your computer. He gave it away free of charge and millions of people downloaded it. The most recent version has been downloaded 24.8 million times from just one website, download.com. Winamp was one of many MP3 players and soon would face stiff competition from Microsoft, RealNetworks, Apple and other big players. But it was Frankel's other innovation—SHOUTcast—that really interests us here.

SHOUTcast is described on its website as "Nullsoft's Free Winamp-based distributed streaming audio system". Simply put, it's the free way to do Internet Radio. The website explains further:

"SHOUTcast is a free-of-charge audio homesteading solution. It permits anyone on the internet to broadcast audio from their PC to listeners across the Internet or any other IP-based network (Office LANs, college campuses, etc.)."

"SHOUTcast's underlying technology for audio delivery is MPEG Layer 3, also known as MP3 technology. The SHOUTcast system can deliver audio in a live situation, or can deliver audio on-demand for archived broadcasts."

SHOUTcast became hugely successful. On a typical Monday morning in November 2004, it was broadcasting over 7,000 radio stations through the net. The most popular of these called itself "Club 977" and played music from the 1980s. It had over 3,500 listeners when I looked, and its maximum listenership had been over 85,000. SHOUTcast claims to broadcast 70 million hours per month of radio content over the net.

Clearly these numbers don't constitute a threat to the giant media monopolies that dominate conventional radio. Nevertheless, they are a huge alternative source of music and information that is completely unregulated and open to all to use at no cost.

In 1999, America Online (AOL) bought Nullsoft, giving it control of both Winamp and SHOUTcast for a reported $100 million.

It was an odd investment, and one wonders what the capitalists at AOL were thinking. (Of course this was the same time as they dreamed up the disastrous merger with Time Warner.) Frankel and his Nullsoft team were mostly giving away Winamp. SHOUTcast was and is free of charge. And even after starting to work for the world's biggest media monopoly (following the merger with Time Warner), Frankel continued with his subversive activities.

He helped create the file sharing program Gnutella, which unlike its forerunner Napster could not be easily brought down by media corporations (such as AOL Time Warner) as it was not so dependent on a central server. AOL made him take it down, but the Gnutella network still exists and is hugely popular.

Frankel then created and distributed a software tool that removed the ads from AOL Instant Messenger. I'm sure his bosses at AOL loved that one too.

Finally, Frankel a bit of code called WASTE. This was a private file-sharing system whose traffic is encrypted. Frankel's idea was that if the giant media companies (AOL Time Warner again) could not see what WASTE users were sharing they couldn't take them to court over copyright infringement.

Amazingly, Frankel remained an employee of AOL Time Warner until early 2004, but the company, angry at these pranks, began to whittle away at his company, Nullsoft. Finally, in November 2004, AOL closed Nullsoft down—putting the future of Winamp and SHOUTcast in doubt.

LIVE 365: RADIO REVOLUTION

Back in July 1999, when Nullsoft first fell into the clutches of AOL, we also saw the launch of possibly the most important company involved in the Internet radio revolution, Live365.

In the beginning, Live365 (http://www.live365.com) offered the possibility of hosting radio stations for free. By early 2001, Live365 was claiming to be hosting no fewer than 25,000 stations. Eventually the company had to start charging to host radio stations, but even with that, it currently hosts several thousand stations and claims over 2,600,000 listeners every month.

We'll come back to Live365 in a later chapter, but suffice it to say here that by offering free, and then low cost, radio stations to anyone who wanted one, Live365 made Internet radio broadcasting possible for thousands of people.

A decade after Rob Glaser first demonstrated streaming multimedia, his company and others (including Nullsoft, Microsoft, Apple, and Live365) had created a technology that would indeed contribute to changing the world.

Reports From the Front Lines

Internet radio sounds like a good idea in theory, but does it work in practice? Can trade unions, environmental organizations, women's groups and community activists make any use of it? The proof is in the practice—in real-world examples of organizations and individuals which follows.

I've selected a few examples from different parts of the world of people and movements using Internet radio. There are many more examples and as more and more of you and your organizations make use of this technology, I'd like to hear about it.

USA: WORKERS INDEPENDENT NEWS SERVICE (WINS)

I first came across the Madison, Wisconsin-based Workers Independent News Service (WINS) at a conference on labor and technology in San Francisco at the end of 2001.

Frank Emspak, the founder of WINS, told the participants about a really exciting new project that was about to be launched. He then played a recording—a demo tape really—to all of us. It was just a brief reading of the news. But the reading was professional. It sounded just like a "real" radio station.

I returned from San Francisco to London and on 20 December 2001 awarded WINS the "labor website of the week", a popular feature on the LabourStart website. I wrote at the time:

"The official launch date may be sometime in January, but I was given a preview of this site and the extraordinary project behind it at the recent LaborTech 2001 conference in San Francisco. WINS aims to eventually provide a daily labor radio broadcast delivered to subscribing radio stations via the Internet, in the form of MP3 files…You can hear a sample broadcast and find out much more by visiting this site."

The intention of WINS, at the time, was not to create an Internet radio station, but to use the internet to deliver content to AM and FM radio stations in the United States.

The WINS website sums up what the project is all about today. It begins by stating the problem:

"Radio is a powerful force. More than 12,000 AM and FM stations broadcast to millions of listeners every day. But too often conservative viewpoints dominate the airwaves while workers' interests are ignored. If you listen to what's considered 'business news' on the radio today, you'll hear lots about stock prices, corporate earnings, and profit/loss ratios—but nothing about the people that make commerce possible."

And then goes on suggest a solution:

"Workers Independent News Service (WINS) gathers news by and about working people and creates programs and feature stories for commercial, public, community and college radio stations throughout the United States."

More than two years after its launch, WINS still didn't seem to be aiming at either an international audience, nor to broadcast to the masses via the net. But it was using the net in an interesting way, by making its content available both to (paying) subscribers and the general public in the form of MP3 files.

Many Internet radio stations start as conventional stations and re-broadcast their content through the net. WINS offers that model in reverse, starting with net-based content that can later be re-broadcast. As we will see later, this model is possibly the most intriguing use of the net for radio broadcasts, particularly in the developing world.

WINS' "mission", say its founders, is to "bring balance to radio news coverage" by providing news and features on the following subjects:

Organizing and bargaining for workplace democracy

Workplace issues: safety, privacy, discrimination

Coalition campaigns for a living wage and other goals

Unions in communities and the political arena

Workforce issues: undocumented workers, contingent and part time workers, immigrant workers

Assistance to local activists

Despite its commitment to a US audience and serving as a channel to conventional radio stations in that country, WINS has expanded to include far more international news—and offers listeners around the globe a chance to hear the broadcasts through the net, via the WINS website at http://www.laborradio.org.

Listeners to WINS will hear a daily 3 minute broadcast, usually read by two newsreaders. The first two minutes consist of a series of short news items, followed by a one minute "Dow Bob" report on some aspect of economic news. In addition, several times a month the service produces feature stories focusing on campaigns, strikes and workplace issues. These also run around three minutes.

WINS also offers subscribers the headline newscast scripts (for publication) and several cartoons each month from labor cartoonist Mike Konopacki (formatted for both online and print publication).

WINS aims to do more than just produce a daily radio show five days a week. It also "offers training and assistance to unions and community-based organizations in the technical aspects of reporting, radio production and media relations. Part of our mission is to help build the capacity of local organizations to speak in their own voices about matters of concern to them."

More than two years into the project, I asked its founder, Frank Emspak, how it was going.

"The project continues to grow," he says. "We have broken through to commercial radio—we are on about 40 stations daily. We are also being broadcast on the largest of the old Pacifica network stations; and Free Speech Radio news also takes features. More unions at both a local and national level are supporting us; some are advertising or sponsoring our program on one station or another. There is also an increasing awareness of our efforts in the labor education and intellectual community-as well as in the news reporter community."

I asked for some more detail about those stations. In addition to the 40 commercial stations, WINS is used by a dozen non-commercial ones, and is re-broadcast by some 60 Free Speech Radio stations as well as some individual programmers on commercial and college radio stations. Low-power FM stations are allowed to use the content free of charge, and WINS doesn't know how many do so. Finally, a handful of Internet-only radio stations also use the content, including Radio LabourStart (more on this later).

No one has any idea how many people actually listen to WINS, but Emspak's best guess is "at least 100,000." But he has no idea how many people listen through the website, downloading the MP3 files which are on offer.

WINS is heavily promoted by American unions. About a third of the unions affiliated to the AFL-CIO have links to WINS on their websites, as well as about a hundred local unions.

Emspak says that WINS aims to be on over 100 commercial stations every day in all major markets in the US. They also hope to feature on major non-commercial stations, have a presence in the college market, and be the supplier of choice of labor news to the low-power FM stations and progressive media in general.

He emphasizes that "as we move toward this goal we want to maintain our commitment to being a voice for the labor and community movement; we want activists in the community and the labor movement to know they will have a place to go that will cover their stories in a honest and forthright manner; we want to maintain our focus on the 'issues and concerns' of working people. As time goes on we want to maintain our editorial independence by maintaining some sort of financial stability—we want to be dependent on the sales to radio stations, the progressive movement, individual local unions and also some donations—in other words we want to achieve financial health from diversified sources."

Emspak sums up saying, "we want to influence the way in which working people approach the media. We hope to encourage a pro-active, issue-centered approach. We want to do all we can to encourage the idea that working people should speak for themselves and that 'media' organizations such as ours can be a vehicle for that speech."

YUGOSLAVIA: RADIO B92

Radio B92 is an example of a how a traditional radio station can use the Internet in moments of crisis (and beyond). Launched in Belgrade in May 1989 at a time when Yugoslavia was still a federation encompassing Serbia, Croatia, Bosnia and so on, it began life as an experimental youth station.

But it quickly grew into something much larger than that, and began broadcasting a mix of news, culture, entertainment and talk shows. It even expanded beyond radio, creating a film and television production division, an Internet service provider, a publishing house, a music label and an "alternative cultural center" known as Cinema Rex. In 1996, it launched a website. The station was hugely popular, and by the time of its tenth anniversary, Radio B92 was the highest-rated station in Belgrade.

It was also involved in setting up ANEM (the Association of Independent Electronic Media), which united more than than 30 independent broadcasters throughout the country.

But Radio B92 was to prove a thorn in Serbian President Slobodan Milosevic's side. It reported on mass demonstrations against the government, triggering two government bans that were quickly lifted following local and international pressure.

The station was banned for a third time on the day that NATO began bombing Belgrade. But despite the ban, Radio B92 continued its existence by broadcasting through the ANEM network—and online.

In April 1999 the government had had enough, and a government-backed group seized control of the station's building and the offices of ANEM as well. The

Radio B92 employees all refused to work for the new station and "regrouped, fighting a rearguard action in private homes," as the station's website now puts it.

Radio B92 began broadcasting using the services of an Internet provider in Amsterdam, xs4all. com.

Milosevic could impose a legal ban, and his goons could seize control of the station's offices and equipment, but he couldn't stop an Internet radio broadcast based in the Netherlands. Ironically, the Serbian dictator would find himself in the Netherlands two years as a prisoner, facing trial at the International Criminal Tribunal for the Former Yugoslavia.

Financial support for the move of Radio B92 to an Internet-only existence was provided in part by the Glaser Progress Foundation, which was set up by Real-Networks founder Rob Glaser.

Only a few months after Radio B92 began its existence as essentially an Internet-only station, it returned to the airwaves in August 1999 as Radio B2-92. By the end of the year, it was back on a full program schedule, even producing films and television programs. At the same time as doing their media work, the station supporters and the whole ANEM network campaigned for press freedom against the increasingly repressive character of the Milosevic regime.

Less than a year before Milosevic's arrest, his regime was still at it, banning Radio B92. But the station was better prepared each time, and within 24 hours of its May 2000 ban, Radio B92 resumed broadcasting news and current affairs programs via the Internet and satellite, again using the ANEM network. Station supporters claim that even under the government ban, by using alternative means it was able to reach at least 60 percent of the country's population.

The Milosevic regime was crumbling, and a few weeks before the dictator's defeat in a presidential election, B92 launched its own television station. Programs were produced in Belgrade and distributed via satellite.

In October 2000, a popular uprising brought an end to the nightmare of Milosevic's rule and the survivors at Radio B92 took control once again of the offices they had used until 1999.

Even though B92 can now freely broadcast inside Serbia using conventional television and radio, the station continues to broadcast content over the net using both the Real and MP3 formats. Its Internet staff consists of six people, and its website, with news in Serbian, Albanian and English, gets more than a quarter of a million page views per day.

GLOBAL: IMC RADIO NETWORK

The IndyMedia websites, scattered around the globe, arose out of the anti-globalization mass protests of the late 1990s. Like the rest of the IndyMedia websites, the Independent Media Centers (IMC) Radio Network site at http://radio. indymedia.org/ is a bit of mess, anarchic, like the anti-globalization movement itself.

The page is divided into four main sections.

First of all, you're invited to join the IMC Audio List if you want to discuss radical radio programming with others. It might be a good idea to sign up for this list.

This is followed by a very prominent link to the A-Infos Radio Project (http://radio4all.net/). This project was founded in 1996 "by grassroots broadcasters, free radio journalists and cyber-activists to provide ourselves with the means to share our radio programs via the Internet," according to the website, which goes on to claim that "the A-Infos Radio Project was the first grassroots media project of its kind on the internet". The project goal is "to support and expand the movement for democratic communications worldwide. We exist to be an alternative to the corporate and government media which do not serve struggles for liberty, justice and peace, nor enable the free expression of creativity".

This is followed by a long list of progressive and community radio stations, many of them broadcasting online. This is a great place to begin looking for such stations, especially as most of the other directories of Internet radio show very few, if any, such stations. The list also includes resources for those groups and individuals contemplating setting up a radio station, online or off.

The second column lists "Current live radio streams as reported to radio. indymedia.org". This is a highly eclectic list, and includes a number of stations that no one seems to be listening to. (It indicates how many listeners a station has at that moment.) For example, San Francisco Liberation Radio doesn't seem to have any listeners at all, nor did Free Radio Santa Cruz. The most popular station when I looked was "rampART radio—revolutionary vibes from east london" which seemed to have five listeners. Nothing for the giant media monopolies to worry about here, then.

The third and fourth columns are lists of audio files available for download. Not strictly speaking Internet radio, but this site like so many others blurs the difference.

Probably the outstanding feature of the IMC Radio Network is what makes the Indymedia sites unique—the ability of anyone visiting the site to upload content. You simply click on the "Publish" link on top of the page, add any text you want, and upload your file and you're done.

The problem with this model, to be honest, is that a lot of garbage gets uploaded to the Indymedia sites.

Nevertheless, a number of alternative broadcasters have used Indymedia as a quick and easy way of getting their material up onto the net. (The A-Infos Radio Project mentioned above plays the same role.)

USA: AIR AMERICA

In early 2004, RealNetwork's Rob Glaser and others raised a reported $60 million to launch a left-wing alternative to the popular right-wing radio programs which had dominated US airwaves throughout the 1990s. Spearheading the effort was comedian and author Al Franken, who became known for a book attacking right-wing radio host Rush Limbaugh.

Air America was not launched as an Internet-only station. Instead, it launched as a conventional 24 hour station on a handful of stations across the US—WLIB-AM in New York, KBLA-AM in Los Angeles, WNTD-AM in Chicago, KPOJ-AM in Portland and KCAA-AM in San Bernardino, California. Some of these were not very powerful stations; the one in New York City, for example, broadcasts only 10,000 watts.

But Air America did embrace some new technology, broadcasting also via satellite, to the three million subscribers to the XM network. By the end of 2004, it had expanded considerably and was broadcasting on 40 local stations across the country. It could now claim to be able to reach some 40% of the country's population. And Air America has plans to expand to hundreds of other, smaller markets.

To reach an even larger audience, Air America now broadcasts through its website, at http://www.airamericaradio.com. "We thought it was very important from day one to be live on the Internet," says AirAmerica Chief Executive Doug Kreeger.

Initially, it only broadcast through RealPlayer, which is not surprising considering Rob Glaser's investment in the project. Today, Air America's live stream can be heard using RealPlayer or Windows Media Player, though oddly enough, it has announced a policy of limiting the time one can listen to the station. After three hours listening, Air America will cut you off, forcing you to reconnect.

The initial experiment with streaming multimedia was a huge success. RealNetworks announced that over two million streams were delivered for Air America Radio through the fledgling website during the network's first week. The station's chairman said that number was a testament to both the quality of the programming—and the "reach of the Real 10 platform". A nice plug for Rob Glaser's company there.

In addition to live broadcasts, Air America takes advantage of something you simply cannot do with traditional radio broadcasts: it allows you to select highlights of previous broadcasts and listen to them at your leisure. When I last looked, these included a program on gay marriage, Al Franken reading aloud from his best-selling book "Lies and the Lying Liars Who Tell Them", and an interview with a freelance journalist based in Baghdad.

Curiously, in spite of Rob Glaser's funding of the project, you cannot listen to the archived material via RealPlayer—it is only being broadcast using Microsoft's Windows Media Player.

USA: BUILDING BRIDGES

Mimi Rosenberg and Ken Nash have been producing "Building Bridges: Your Community and Labor Report" for WBAI radio in New York City for several years now. The show airs on FM radio but has long had an Internet component as well. I asked Ken to describe how the show uses the net.

"We send out links to a national version (30 minute) of our show to our [mailing] list and it is sometimes picked up by other listserves on a sporadic basis, depending on the subject. We also do postings on about 20 Indymedia sites a week. Posting it on these sites often gets the show individual listings on the web so when I do a Google search for our show, many of these postings show up. We are also able to give a link to radio4all [the A-Infos Radio Project]—where we post the show—for a combined listing of all our posted shows." Ken adds that Building Bridges also posts frequently on sites related to subjects they broadcast about, and on LabourStart, the global online labor news service, where Ken serves as a volunteer correspondent.

In addition to making Building Bridges available on other sites, WBAI also streams the show through its own website, though Ken adds that it "would be a great benefit if WBAI shows were archived as KPFA does" with its shows. (KPFA is a sister station of WBAI.)

Despite all these efforts to use the net to expand the audience for the show, Ken remains skeptical. "It is difficult to assess how effective this all is," he says. "Of course it goes out nationally and internationally, but we get very little feedback. I think there is a resistance to listening on the web which I don't really understand. A few years back this was understandable because many computers were not adapted for listening."

But there was one moment when Ken became convinced of the power of Internet radio. "Back when the big fight occurred for control of Pacifica and WBAI, internet radio (both a station that was created called radio in exile, and postings) played a huge role in the struggle because many of us were off the air and also we were able to document and replay what was being done with the airtime."

USA: JIM HIGHTOWER

Jim Hightower describes himself as "America's #1 Populist" on his website, located at http://www.jimhightower.com.

Hightower will be a familiar figure to anyone active on the American left. He's the author of several books with great titles such as "If the Gods Had Meant Us To Vote, They Would Have Given Us Candidates" and "There's Nothing In the Middle Of the Road But Yellow Stripes and Dead Armadillos." He's also done something remarkable: won elections in Texas running on an explicitly anti-corporate platform.

Hightower is also an important figure in the development of Internet radio. If I had to think of the first time I heard progressives using streaming audio over the net, it would probably be Jim Hightower.

His website is the place to go to hear his daily two-minute commentary on current affairs, broadcast in Real format only. In addition to offering the audio, Hightower provides a written transcript as well. The most recent broadcast of his that I heard was an appeal to progressive Americans not to leave the US for Canada in the wake of the Bush victory in November 2004.

"Karl Rove would like nothing more than to see all of us move away, leaving America to him," says Hightower in his inimitable Texas drawl. "We have no right to do anything like that—it's our happy duty to be in their face and take our country back."

The broadcast is also aired on over a hundred US local radio stations.

One of the great things about the Hightower website—and here's clear advantage of Internet radio over any other kind—is that he has what appears to be a complete archive of his two-minute shows, going back more than a decade. The very earliest ones go back to February 1993. Clearly these were not broadcast in Real format back then, but have obviously been rescued from the archives and made available to listeners now.

In that first broadcast I could find, Hightower is attacking the North American Free Trade Agreement.

"So let's ask ourselves: NAFTA—do we hafta? No. Not this treaty. I've read it—all 2000 pages. It'll just make it easier for auto companies, banking, electronics, food processing, and dozens of other corporations to abandon U.S. communities…and exploit Mexican communities. This thing's so ugly it'd rot a cantaloupe at 100 paces."

A recording like that one is absolutely precious—and thanks to the net, preserved so that we can hear it today.

Another advantage of putting audio content on the net is that Hightower is able to reach a large number of people who are not within range of those US radio stations. This would include millions of people around the world who would be astonished to discover that there are people like Hightower in a place like Texas. (Though of course the Dixie Chicks probably have already made that point to a larger audience.)

Hightower's daily commentary shows how one man can use Internet radio to change the world.

USA: RADIO NATION

Marc Cooper is the host of this online radio station which is associated with the venerable US progressive magazine, The Nation. The Nation has been doing online broadcasts since 1995, and its radio website can be found at http://www.thenation.com/blogs/audioblog/

The format of the website is actually rather different from what we have come to expect. It appears to be a weblog (blog), but instead of reading content, one listens. Radio Nation is using a new service (launched in May 2004) called AudioBlog and it promises to be an easy and inexpensive way for organizations and individuals to get audio content up on the net. This makes the site easy to use, but it also means that the archive seems to go back only to July 2004.

Recent stories aired by Cooper focus on the US elections (an interview with historian Howard Zinn), Putin's Russia, Chile, and much more. They often feature interviews with prominent figures on the American left, such as Gore Vidal, Jonathan Schell, and Norman Lear.

The Nation's audio content is also delivered a large number of conventional radio stations throughout the US—and even a station in Costa Rica.

KOREA: FREE NK

North Korean defectors based in Seoul, South Korea, have launched an Internet radio station to promote democracy in the world's most closed society. The station is located on the web at http://www.freenk.net.

Before saying another word, I should point out that North Korea is probably the most repressive society on the planet. No dissident voices of any kind are tolerated and the ruling Stalinist regime completely controls all media.

According to Amnesty International, "Political opposition of any kind was not tolerated. According to reports, any person who expressed an opinion contrary to the position of the ruling Korean Workers' Party faced severe punishment, and so did their family in many cases. The domestic news media continued to be strictly censored and access to international media broadcasts was restricted."

The international organization Reporters Without Borders ranked North Korea in last place in its list of countries in order of press freedom—for three years in a row.

Of course other countries such as the US and South Korea are trying to break through that censorship with radio and television broadcasts, using Voice of America (VOA) and Radio Free Asia. The South Korean radio stations KBS and Keuk-dong are also said to be popular.

But as a Reporters Without Borders report made clear, until recently "what was missing was a radio station run by members of the North Korean community living in the South. The creation of the Seoul-based FreeNK with radio programs on its website…has filled the gap."

FreeNK'sInternet radio broadcasts began in April 2004 with the words: "Hello. We're starting up Free NK from today from Seoul, the capital of the Republic of Korea. Toward freedom, democracy and unification."

The first broadcast mentioned the remarks made by the official media in the Communist state concerning the impeachment of South Korea's president. "If democratic politics could be realized in the North as it is in the South," the broadcasters said, "one would have to recognize that the nation, its leaders and the Workers Party would have been impeached hundreds of times over."

The station's studio was initially located on the sixth floor of the building of the Institute of North Korean Studies in Seoul, which had given it a free, six-month lease. The Institute was founded as an affiliate agency of the National Intelligence Service in 1971 and privatized in 1993.

According to a report in a South Korean newspaper announcing the launch of the service, the voices of the two female broadcasters (whose real names were not given) were "strong and emotionally-charged" and that they spoke in a way that was "characteristic of North Korean speech patterns".

One of the broadcasters had ten year's experience in broadcasting as a member of a provincial propaganda brigade in North Korea. Right after high school, she was selected to become a broadcaster because of her forceful voice. For 10 years she drove around in a specially designed car to towns "introducing stories to force people to worship [North Korean dictator] Kim Jung-il."

"As I can now deliver the true stories about the North to listeners, I hope that the program will help people in North Korea know the reality of the their government," she said.

Asked why they spoke in a typically North Korean way, one replied: "Well, we can do it well, and we think that way of speaking, which is familiar to North Korean citizens and defectors living abroad, is better. If we try to imitate South Korean announcers, well, firstly, we don't have the skills to do so, and people might mistakenly believe that these broadcasts are not being made by defectors themselves."

The station was created by its president, Lee Sung-min, a seven-man editorial staff, a skills coach, announcers, reporters and web specialists. All of them are North Korean defectors.

The start-up costs of the project were W30 million (about $25,000), which they were able to get through personal donations from members of a 4,000-strong domestic defector organization.

Live broadcasts lasted for one hour, from 8:00 PM to 9:00 PM every evening, but the website also featured recorded materials.

The station's schedule included daily news under the headline "North-South Relations News" and a daily program about the experience of defectors called "Defector Notes". There were also weekly broadcasts, including former North Korean Workers (Communist) Party Secretary Hwang Jang-yeop's "Democratic Philosophy Classes," Chungang University Professor Kim Yong-beom's "The Structure of National Division and North Korean Literature" and even "North Korean Poetry and Songs." Once a week, one of the station's seven editors would read an editorial statement on North Korean affairs as well.

"Our program aims to help North Koreans know better about their actual situation and to let the rest of world know about the reality of the North Korean government. (Our aim is also) to finally lead the nation to become a democratic nation like South Korea," said one of the station's founders. Station founder Kim, now 44 years old, in 1999 became the first North Korean writer to defect to the South.

Noh Yu-jin is one of two hosts of Free North Korea Broadcasting and is in charge of delivering the news stories. Every show begins with Noh reading the following: "We will devote ourselves to spreading the idea of freedom and democracy to North Koreans until the day of reunification of the two Koreas. We will be like a lighthouse of hope for people in North Korea and a torchlight of truth for people in South Korea."

Chong Chu-han, the show's other host, reads out editorials written by professors and other experts on North Korea, as well as poems dealing with the North.

In its first few weeks online, 3,000 people joined the station as members and 10,000 logged in every day thereafter.

It quickly got itself into hot water as Hwang Jang-yeop harshly criticized the Communist regime in a broadcast right after the massive explosion in the North Korean city of Ryongchon on April 22.

By 8 May, the Institute which owned the building from which the broadcasts were made suspended the station's lease, ordering "FreeNK" out by the end of the month.

According to a South Korean press report, the Institute claimed that "bad people might launch a terrorist attack or cause a disturbance"—and asked the station to leave.

It was reported that the North Korean-linked "National Democratic Front of South Korea" threatened to "blow up the criminals' cyber-broadcasting site and kill the dirty traitors."

A guard at the Institute building said that "strange people" would come by to protest on a daily basis against the hosting of the radio station. Threatening emails and phone calls have also reached the North Korean defectors involved in running the station.

Station chief Kim Seong-min has been called a "traitor" and told, "you'd better be careful—I won't let you get away with this."

The activities of the radio station were repeatedly raised by North Korean government officials in inter-ministerial talks with the South Korean government.

The South Korean newspaper Chosun Ilbo noted the irony: "Since it was an Internet broadcasting system, people in North Korea couldn't even listen to it."

This is not entirely true. The defectors planned to provide their contents to other international stations which could be heard in part of North Korea such as Voice of America, Radio Free Asia and the Far East Broadcasting Corporation.

"The VOA has already started airing some parts of our program," said Kim, "and I think North Korean residents will be able to listen to our program if we can improve the quality of the reporting, because then other international stations would be willing to use our material in their own programs."

Very quickly, the station made enemies both of the North Korean regime and those in the South who "blindly believe in North-South reconciliation"—including those businesses currently investing millions in the North.

Chosun Ilbo bemoans the fact that "the defectors' lessons are quietly slipping away. In the fate of Free NK Radio is the reality that even the faintest of defector voices now have a difficult time finding space for themselves in this land."

Workers at the radio station, who are all volunteers, said that harassment of their shoestring operation drew neither government condemnation nor police protection.

Emboldened by the eviction of the radio station, North Korea's news agency demanded that the South Korean government also stop tours of the infamous "invasion tunnels" dug by the North Korean army under the demilitarized zone in the 1970s.

Today FreeNK has found new quarters, and is now guarded by a policeman. It continues to broadcast through the web.

Radio LabourStart

In my book, *The labour movement and the Internet: The new internationalism*, written back in 1996, I concluded with what I called "three crazy ideas". I wasn't being modest or anything; the ideas really were crazy. At the time.

The first of them was "an online international labor press." Back in the mid-1990s, the closest thing to an international labor press would have been the magazines published by the International Confederation of Free Trade Unions (ICFTU) and the international trade secretariats (now known as global union federations). Chances are you never saw any of these publications. They all had very limited circulations. All the average member of a trade union ever heard from the international labor movement was what his or her national union would copy and put into the union magazine they'd receive in the post.

I was proposing something truly different: an online international labor press. I began by describing the sorry state of the labor press in different countries, including the U.S. I suggested that the Internet offered a solution: the creation of a daily online labor news service or newspaper. I even suggested that the notion of it being a daily was irrelevant. It could be updated continuously throughout the day. To make it clear to readers what I was talking about, I described such a publication as "a series of pages on the World Wide Web."

I went further and suggested that such an online labor publication would have to be multilingual from the start. I urged that it be launched in the all the major European languages, as well as Chinese, Korean, Japanese and Arabic.

Finally, I suggested that such an online labor newspaper would help create a "community of ideas and feelings among its readers." It would be, I argued, "the best organizing tool ever in the hands of the international labor movement." It should be launched without delay, I concluded.

As an afterthought—maybe because the idea of an online daily labor newspaper in all the major languages sounded Utopian enough—I tagged on this:

"[A] daily online labor newspaper is only the beginning of what might be done. The latest technological developments are truly stunning—'streaming multimedia' on the net. These applications basically turn the Internet into a full-blown, real-time global radio and television broadcast medium that also happens to be interactive.

"Using an ordinary home computer, equipped with a not-very-fast modem, a couple of inexpensive speakers and a sound card, I have been able to listen in on some local radio broadcasts from around the world. Using a technology like Real-Audio (the client program as well as the encoder are available free of charge), it would be fairly easy to launch what was once an impossible dream: a global labor radio network."

As I said, a pretty crazy idea. Especially back in 1996. Realizing that I needed to explain further, to make it sound even remotely credible, I continued:

"The labor movement wouldn't need expensive broadcasting equipment nor governmental permission to 'broadcast' using a technology of this kind. Such broadcasts could be picked up by trade unionists anywhere in the world, and could be copied and re-broadcast using conventional local radio stations in places where Internet access is expensive. Such broadcasts (actually 'narrowcasts' is a better term) are much harder to censor or jam than ordinary radio.

"More advanced Internet technologies available today, such as VDOLive, offer the promise of live television broadcasts (though these do not work with slow modems). Inexpensive color digital video cameras (which currently cost about the same as a 28,800 bps modem) mean that online labor television broadcasts are only a matter of time. The possibilities for the international trade union movement are staggering indeed."

I suggested that such a daily labor online newspaper be produced by the ICFTU and the global union federations. They, however, did not take up my suggestion. (Though the launch of the Global Unions website at http://www.global-unions.org several years later was a step in that direction.) The idea of a global labor radio station through the Internet was somewhat ahead of its time.

Looking back at what I wrote, I can see that the LabourStart web project (http://www.labourstart.org) which I launched after the book's publication did realize many the ambitions I set for this "crazy idea". LabourStart was initially just part of the website I created to accompany the publication of "The Labour Movement and the Internet: The New Internationalism". My idea had been that the book would quickly be out of date (how right I was!) and we'd need a way to keep readers informed of changes, such as new trade union websites or mailing lists.

I convinced my publisher to even include—discretely placed at the very bottom of the contents page—a hyper-link to the page on the free GeoCities website where I would provide "updates and corrections" to the book.

It quickly became much more than that, first hosting a daily English language news service reporting on the dramatic strikes taking place in South Korea, and then from March 1998 onwards, reporting on global labor news under the name "LabourStart: Where trade unionists start their day on the net."

I won't bore you with the details of LabourStart's history, save to point out that it eventually evolved into what is probably the most popular trade union website in the world, with a network of nearly 300 volunteer correspondents providing the news, which appears in 15 different language editions and which is syndicated to over 500 trade union websites. Within just a couple of years of the publication of "The labour movement and the Internet: The new internationalism" a global labor online newspaper had become a reality.

But a radio station—that still seemed pretty Utopian.

I should backtrack a bit and in the interests of historical accuracy point out that the idea of a global labor radio station is not something I thought up in a moment of inspired creativity. It is something that I once read about. Apparently back in the 1920s, the international trade union movement and the social democratic parties which were its close political allies, did explore the possibility of just such a project. That was a time when radio was increasingly being used by the world's great powers to get their message out. For practical reasons, the project never got off the ground, and as far as I know, no further attempt was made.

I read about that decades ago and never forgot it—it captured my imagination. As a regular listener to some of the more successful global radio stations, and in particular the BBC World Service with its tens of millions of listeners, I thought it would be absolutely fantastic if an alternative station could be launched, one expressing the views and the vision of the democratic labor movement.

And for several years after the launch of LabourStart, I thought about attempting something like this myself. After all, how hard could it be to launch an online radio station?

I read about Live365 which allowed anyone to register and use its technology to broadcast radio via the net, completely free of charge. I signed up—and like most of the people who did so, promptly forgot all about it. I never used my account and let it lapse.

But the idea of a global labor radio station was always in the back of my mind and I thought that if no one else does it, LabourStart, which by 2004 had become quite a large project, should throw its weight behind it.

In early January 2004, a quiet time when many trade unionists are still off on their winter holidays (and those in Australia and New Zealand are beginning their summer breaks), I had the free time to once again see what was on offer if I wanted to launch an Internet radio station. I found that in 2004, as in the past, Live365 dominated the field—but was no longer free.

Later on in this book I'll tell you all about how one goes about setting up an Internet radio station and what it costs, but suffice it say that I discovered in early 2004 that it was dead easy to set up, and didn't cost very much money.

I notified all of LabourStart's correspondents that we'd begin trial broadcasts that very month, and would go live with a public announcement on 1 February 2004—designed to coincide with the announcement of the winner of our annual Labor Website of the Year competition, to ensure a maximum number of responses.

Basically, in order to launch the station we needed content. Most of the stations on Live365 broadcast recorded music, using playlists. There are other approaches. One could do live broadcasts, but this costs more and requires that someone be sitting at a microphone. Recorded playlists sounded like the way to go.

The content would therefore have to be a mix of music and talk. And talk meant getting labor news from somewhere.

Fortunately, the Workers Independent News Service (WINS) came to our rescue. They offered us free use of their service, which meant a 3 minute news summary every day, including their "Dow Bob" report, as well as access to their features.

Getting the WINS content—which they normally charge for—was also quite easy, once we had a user ID and password. I'd simply log-in to their website and download their news as an MP3 file.

Getting the content up onto Live365's servers was also simple enough. They provide a free bit of software called Studio365 which allows you to upload files to their server, and to sort those out in playlists, and much more.

Later in the book, I'll tell you in greater detail how all this works (for you to use when setting up your own Internet radio station) but the point being that no special technical skills are required, software is all free, and from the moment you think you might want to do an Internet radio station until it's actually on the air can be a matter of minutes.

Daily trial broadcasts began on 26 January 2004, and they were listened to by LabourStart correspondents and individuals who may have stumbled on the site through Live365's directory. On our best day during that first week we had five listeners in 24 hours.

On Sunday, 1 February 2004, we launched Radio LabourStart with a mass mailing to our 18,000 or so email subscribers—a mailing which was primarily designed to announce the winner of the Labor Website of the Year competition. We added:

"We're also announcing today the launch of our brand-new radio station, Radio LabourStart, which began broadcasting 24 hours a day, 7 days a week on the Internet.

"Radio LabourStart contains a mix of news, views and 'songs to fan the flames of discontent'. Today's show is playing Woody Guthrie singing his classic 'This Land is Your Land', Bob Dylan's 'Blowing in the Wind', Pete Seeger's rendition of 'Casey Jones (The Union Scab)', Bruce Springsteen's 'Ghost of Tom Joad', and many more. Today and every day of the week our broadcast includes the 3-minute labor news report produced by the Workers Independent News Service (WINS).

"If you have a sound card and speakers on your PC, and an Internet connection, you can start listening today to our regular daily one hour broadcasts. You can also learn more about this very exciting project and find out how you can be part of it, here: http://radio.laborstart.org/'"

Note the reference to daily one-hour broadcasts. That meant a one-hour long playlist, consisting of 3 minutes of news and 57 minutes of music, repeated throughout the day.

Not anticipating very many listeners at first, we had purchased one of Live365's cheapest hosting packages, which allowed us up to 50 simultaneous listeners. Knowing that we'd have listeners spread around the world in different time zones, we had to assume that 50 would certainly be enough for any given moment.

But within a day or two of the station's launch, Live365's website was telling us that 60 people were simultaneously attempting to listen as hundreds of trade unionists attempted to listen to the station. Over 340 people listened in the first 48 hours. We were compelled to upgrade our hosting package within 24 hours of announcing the station's launch—which also gave us much more storage room for our audio files on Live365's servers.

This meant that we could include more music, and were able to move toward a playlist that lasted 90 minutes rather than an hour.

And the reaction of listeners was great—very encouraging.

A trade unionist from the U.S. wrote, "All of us in our family (wife and 10 y.o. son) LOVE the new Live365 radio station! My son doesn't understand why we can't get it on the radio!"

The noted labor educator and union Internet pioneer, Marc Belanger, who now works for the International Labor Organization in Turin, Italy, wrote: "And out of the studios of Eric Lee comes one more advancement in labor communications: radio! Congratulations. I'm glad you're on our side."

A Danish trade unionist wrote: "I have just tuned in to Radio LabourStart. Congratulations. It is fine that workers songs and songs of labor can be heard."

A Canadian unionist added: "I like the labor radio concept, there is a need for a socially progressive alternative to the slop that is generally available on commercial radio."

And so on.

But not all the feedback was positive. Many visitors to the Live365 site were confused about how to listen. Live365 encourages visitors to download their own software (Player365), while in fact you can listen to the station using almost any software that plays MP3 files, including the software that came with your Windows computer. For many of the trade unionists trying to listen to Radio LabourStart, it was their first attempt to hear Internet radio—and it was not as user-friendly as we would have liked.

There were also complaints about the content—especially when the daily playlist was only one hour long. (It's now up to over four hours.)

But after a short while, the number of listeners began to drop off. To keep a steady stream of new listeners coming to the station, we took advantage of Google's keyword based advertisements. This is a way to attract people who are already looking for certain terms on the web and bring them over to listen to the radio station. We used the names of many of the performers whose music we would be playing on Radio LabourStart. So if you searched on Google for, say, "Woody Guthrie" (the great American folksinger) you'd see a small ad displayed in the upper right corner of the page, just opposite the main search results, telling you to click there to hear Woody Guthrie's songs.

In the first seven months of the Google ads being shown, the ads were displayed a staggering 2.3 million times, at a cost of only $700. Over 14,300 visitors were attracted to the radio station (that's around 2,000 per month) while searching for Bob Dylan or Phil Ochs or Joan Baez.

As a result of that publicity, and repeated mailings to LabourStart's list, Radio LabourStart has continued to feature in the top 5% of Live365's 22,000 radio stations.

I should say a word about the music we're playing. Most of the online radio stations I've seen are playing variations on the popular music you can hear on most commercial radio stations. One of the popular Live365 stations is devoted entirely to the Beatles—but you can hear Beatles music played on many AM and FM stations as well. The most popular stations seem to be the ones playing music from specific periods—for example, popular music from the 1980s.

But the radio stations of progressive organizations can play a different role. We can choose to use the new medium of Internet radio to revive the counter-culture of our movement, a culture of our own which counterposes itself to the commercial culture that is owned and controlled by giant corporations.

It was this idea of finding an authentic music that led a generation or two ago to the revival of folk music, and one might add—to the emergence of rock. People grow tired of the same sterile commercial garbage played on most radio stations. Internet radio can bring back to life the sounds of a different culture.

Radio LabourStart's playlists include a whole range of performers some of whom you will probably recognize such as Bob Dylan, Joan Baez, Woody Guthrie, Bruce Springsteen, Pete Seeger, Billy Bragg, perhaps Phil Ochs.

But I'll bet you've never heard of most of these artists—Faith Petric, Robb Johnson, Bob Bovee, Fred Holstein, Jeff Cahill, Martin Whelan, Pierre Fournier, Si Kahn, Utah Phillips, or Zahava Seewald. Yet their music is the authentic music of protest. They sing about the things that matter. And they continue a tradition of alternative, working-class music that goes back to Joe Hill and the Wobblies, and beyond.

We do play music by people you know—but not the songs you may be familiar with. For example, Radio LabourStart is playing a whole bunch of songs sung by Barbra Streisand. Long before Streisand soared to super-stardom she performed in a Broadway musical written by, and mostly performed by, members of the International Ladies Garment Workers Union. The show was called "Pins and Needles" and you can hear Streisand as you've never heard her before (or since) singing songs like "It's Better with a Union Man", "Not Cricket to Picket" and "One Big Union for Two".

Everyone knows the music of John Lennon, but in addition to writing some great love songs, John had an incredibly sharp eye for the issues of social class, having grown up in Liverpool. His song "Working Class Hero" probably doesn't get a lot of play on American radio stations because of lyrics like these—

Keep you doped with religion and sex and TV
And you think you're so clever and classless and free
But you're still fucking peasants as far as I can see
A working class hero is something to be

Not all the music comes from professional musicians. We've been playing lots of music performed by working people themselves. From Canada we received CDs and play music from the Steelworkers Canada Chorus and the Winnipeg Labour Choir. From New Zealand, we have songs from a women's trade union choir in Wellington with the name Choir, Choir, Pants on Fire. In Australia, the Sydney Trade Union Choir sent us a CD of their songs which are now on our playlist too.

The Congress of South African Trade Unions (COSATU) produced a CD of live concert performed at one of its congresses. It's an extraordinary collection of the songs of the African working class—but you won't hear it on conventional radio stations.

We even have versions of the old anthem of the international working class, "The Internationale", sung in ten languages, played throughout the week.

People are writing in and saying that so much of this music is stuff they have never heard before—and so much of it is incredibly powerful. Phil Ochs does a live version of the song "Joe Hill" that will move you to get up out of your chair and go organize workers somewhere. Bruce Springsteen's "Ghost of Tom Joad" makes John Steinbeck sound like a twenty-first century writer confronting the era of globalization and neo-liberalism. Billy Bragg performs an irreverent version of "The Internationale".

All this music, all of it, is utterly subversive. Listen to this music and you'll want to change the world. And that's the whole point of the station.

In addition to all the music, Radio LabourStart has featured a whole range of other content. After union pioneer Victor Reuther (one of the Reuther brothers who founded the United Auto Workers) passed away, we obtained a recording of the memorial service and played that over the course of a weekend. We ran coverage of giant union-led demonstrations in Germany—including recordings made in the field of interviews with protesters. We used Radio LabourStart to build support for several of the online campaigns LabourStart has run. We did a recorded interview with an American university professor who was organizing the world's first-ever global labor survey.

In its first ten months online, Radio LabourStart has been a success—but not a runaway success.

The main problems include the continuing difficulty trade unionists have with figuring out how to listen—even though we have created pages on the website explaining what they need to do. It's not as simple as clicking on a link and visiting a web page.

Another problem is the lack of original content. There are even fewer producers of original audio content than there are listeners for that content. Ideally, an online trade union radio station should feature interviews with the men and women on the picket lines, at trade union conferences, and in the workplace.

Unlike the news service on LabourStart which is in 15 languages, Radio LabourStart continues to appear only in English—though it features music in many other languages. This limits its audience mainly to English speakers.

But worst of all is the fact that it's not being imitated. Imitation is the highest form of flattery, and innovators need to be flattered. LabourStart has demonstrated the viability and do-ability of such a radio station—but unions have not rushed to copy it.

Changing the World

After reading through the last few pages, you might reach the conclusion that this is all very nice and very interesting—but what does it have to do with changing the world?

You might be thinking that you really do need to set up your PC to listen to some of these stations. Maybe you'd like to hear Jim Hightower bashing George Bush in an authentic Texas accent. Or you want to hear John Lennon as you've never heard him before, singing about the dead-end life of working class people as he saw it growing up in Liverpool. Or you want to hear Air America but you're not one of the lucky people living in a major "market" so you can't get it on your radio.

Maybe you've moved beyond that and you're thinking, my union could use a technology like this. Or my environmental group, or my community, or my political network. This would be a good addition to our website, could be the next step for us. It's not expensive, it sounds easy to set up, we should try it.

But you still think that the idea that Internet radio might change the world is going a bit too far.

This is the part of the book where we find out if the author really does have a vision, or as a former US president so eloquently put it, a "vision thing".

I think that if we look just slightly over the horizon, we can begin to see the fantastic potential of this new technology. In this final chapter, I want to focus on a few of those over-the-horizon aspects of Internet radio. In the end I hope you'll agree with me that this is a very special technology, one that can indeed contribute to changing the world.

In attempting to define Internet radio at the beginning of this book, I tried to distinguish it from merely putting up audio files on one's own website. And then

I seemed to contradict that by including among examples of Internet radio stations such things as the Workers Independent News Service (WINS) or Radio Nation, which do exactly that. Despite the name, one doesn't tune in to Radio Nation and listen to it in the background while doing the dishes. It doesn't work that way. What many of the Internet radio broadcasters are doing is creating content, putting it on the web, and then allowing broadcasters of traditional radio stations to transmit the content in a more conventional way.

To take the example of WINS, they are using the power of MP3 files and a website to prepare unique, daily content about working people and their unions which is then broadcast via several dozen radio stations. They are also allowing Internet-only stations, such as Radio LabourStart, to use their content as well.

I think that there is enormous potential here in creating such hybrid radio stations, particularly when it comes to developing countries.

We should never forget that the vast majority of people on the planet do not now have access to the Internet and are not likely to have access at any time in the near future. It's all very well and good to talk about getting broadband ADSL access and buying a decent set of stereo headphones but all this is meaningless if you live in a village without electricity.

But if organizations committed to social change were to produce high-quality content and distribute it via the web—like WINS or Radio Nation or Jim Hightower—that content could be picked up by conventional radio stations in developing countries and re-broadcast. Even areas of the world that don't have electricity often have battery-powered (or even wind-up) radios.

The content would have to be useful and relevant to those people, so obviously the examples I'm giving of US-based content aimed primarily at US audiences is not what we need. If you really want to reach people via radio in the developing world, you have to create content in languages they can understand. And the vast majority of them do not understand English.

Thinking about how the international trade union movement might be doing this, I can imagine the regional organizations which already exist in Asia, Africa and Latin America, organizations which already use the Internet and have modern computer, making the investment in a decent microphone and starting to record content. Then they would have to make the kinds of connections with radio stations throughout those regions to offer them content—for example, news like the kind of news that WINS creates for an American audience.

The best place to create that content and to build those connections is in the regions themselves, and not from the central offices of the global unions in Geneva and Brussels.

When I first discussed this idea nearly a decade ago with an official of the London-based International Transport Workers Federation (ITF), he said it reminded him of an old project to send cassettes with recorded content to developing countries. Those could then be replayed via radio, or in battery-powered portable cassette players.

He pointed something out which I hadn't even thought of: with hundreds of millions of the world's poor and working people being illiterate, audio content could play a role that books and newspapers and websites never could. For unions to reach out to the millions of illiterate workers, many of them working in the informal sector, the majority of them women, using audio might be the best way. And to deliver audio content over a vast region like Africa or Asia, what better way than via the web to local radio stations?

That having been said, I still think that Internet radio in its purest form consists of a stream of content. When one tunes into a true Internet radio station, one should catch a song being played in the middle. That sense of hearing something played live to you (and indeed live broadcasts are the best way to do this) is something special which we should not lose sight of.

The radio stations described earlier, and in particular Radio LabourStart, don't do live broadcasts. They rely on playlists of recorded content. A Radio LabourStart playlist is likely to consist of about four hours of recorded music, interrupted every hour by a three minute labor news summary from WINS.

When you tune into a station like that, you listen as you would to a normal radio station—in the background, while doing something else, occasionally focusing when a particular song or news summary comes on.

It's a different thing entirely when you listen to something like Jim Hightower or Building Bridges. Once you've launched the broadcast, knowing that it only lasts a few minutes and consists entirely of people talking, it grabs your full attention.

Both kinds of Internet radio make sense, and their integration—for example the inclusion of WINS into Radio LabourStart playlists—seems to be the way to go.

Moving toward the model of "live" broadcasts, with a continuously playing stream of music and talk, does lead inevitably to the question of really live broadcasts.

Live365 and the other models do offer this as an option, though because they are bandwidth-intensive, it costs a bit more. Nevertheless, we could switch at any moment on Radio LabourStart from our pre-recorded broadcast to a live one. And this opens up entirely new possibilities for Internet radio.

One of the most popular radio formats in the world these days, and not only in the US, is talk radio. In the US, talk radio is closely associated with the Right and some of its most popular hosts, such as Rush Limbaugh, have been strong supporters of George Bush. Radio stations like Air America were specifically launched to counter right-wing dominated talk radio.

Can you do talk radio over the net? Of course you can. When we first started Radio LabourStart, I needed to record a couple of short interviews over the phone. But I couldn't figure out technically what was needed to accomplish this. I searched Google, but obviously wasn't using very good search terms. Finally, I popped into the local electronics store and to my amazement was shown the simplest of cables that connected a phone to a PC. I plugged in the cable and, voila, was able to record phone calls. It couldn't have been simpler.

To do a live talk show on the net wouldn't require much more than that. Listeners could phone in using conventional phones, just as you would with ordinary talk radio. The difference is, their voices would be heard around the world.

Live Internet radio broadcasts open up another possibility: live reports from the field, just as one can see today on CNN or hear on the BBC World Service.

Practically, probably the best way to do live reports via an Internet radio station is to use mobile phones in the field to call in reports which are then streamed through a server. We could do this today on Radio LabourStart at no cost. Any campaigning organization can do this tomorrow at very low cost.

All of this leads us to an extraordinary possibility. Imagine you're at a demonstration somewhere. There are tens of thousands of people around. You want to know what is happening. You could listen to your portable transistor radio, where government-regulated, commercially-sponsored stations may or may not tell you the news you need to know.

Some organizations have gotten around this problem by an imaginative use of SMS short text messages to mobile phones. During a huge lobby of the British Parliament by drop-the-debt campaigners, this proved to be an effective means of communicating with the protesters. But SMS messages are very short and that's a serious limitation.

But imagine if you could listen through a device the size of a portable transistor radio to live Internet radio? In that case, the organizers of the event—the union or campaigning organization—can broadcast directly, in real-time, to participants in the protest, telling them of any developments they need to know about.

Such devices already exist in the form of "smart phones" and handheld computers (such as the Palm or Pocket PC). The missing link is a high-speed Internet connection which can be picked up wirelessly, like a transistor radio. But those high-speed wireless networks are becoming a reality in the centers of many big cities. Using a technology known as Wi-Fi, small handheld computers can receive broadcasts. Software exists which allows them to listen to Internet radio.

I have a Palm handheld—a year-old model called a Tungsten C. It comes with a built-in receiver for wireless Internet connections. I have installed a bit of software on it to play MP3 music called Pocket Tunes. Pocket Tunes allows me to listen to Internet radio stations broadcast via SHOUTcast. If I were in an area covered by a wireless network, I could listen to Radio LabourStart through headphones—just as one might listen to an ordinary transistor radio. The difference is that I'd have access to tens of thousands of radio stations, including stations that challenged the ruling elites and that represented popular movements.

I hope you're now getting a sense of how far we can go with Internet radio. Using cellphones and wireless networks, we can go far beyond the model of someone broadcasting from a studio to someone sitting at a desktop PC. We can move toward a model of activists in the field relaying content to other activists through wireless networks and streaming multimedia. And we can do it all at very low cost.

But the really exciting thing to me about the new technology, as I wrote at the very beginning of the book, is its global dimension. If you're thinking about using Internet radio to support a community organization or a trade union branch, that's fine. But we should also be thinking how we can use the new technology to build global actions and a global consciousness.

Let's take Radio LabourStart as an example. The website it grew out of appears in fifteen languages and has volunteer correspondents on every continent. They update the site continuously through the day. While the Australians are sleeping, the correspondents in Europe and Africa are adding new content to the site, and as they start heading home from their offices, the North Americans come online and begin adding content.

Now imagine the same scenario played through the radio station. It could be possible to set up a series of playlists aimed at particular time zones. At 09:00 GMT, when Europeans are first coming to work, there could be a European focus. Eight hours later, as they head home, it would be noon on the east coast of North America, and 9:00 AM on the west coast—a good time to start broadcasts aimed at that audience. And so on as the day progresses.

Let's think about how we'd do that with live broadcasts. We could have hosts scattered around the globe, each one coming online at a certain time and taking over the broadcast. Imagine at 17:00 GMT, in the example I just gave, a host in London signing off and passing on the broadcast to one in Vancouver, who would be followed eight hours later by one in Sydney.

And there's no reason to stick with eight-hour slots. Why not have 24 different slots, 24 different hosts, each one broadcasting labor news relevant to that part of the world (including global labor news of course), playing music from a particular region, and so on?

To a certain extent, this is what some of the big global media players like CNN already do. But it can also be done cheaply and easily using readily available tools like Live365.

And if that's not exciting enough (I think it's pretty exciting, but what do I know?)—there's the next obvious step: internet TV.

The first efforts to create streaming video online were catastrophes. Anyone who tried RealVideo when it first came out in 1997 saw tiny, grainy images for a few seconds before buffering problems removed even those. The improved software and more important, the ready availability of high-speed broadband access, has completely changed the picture.

Not long ago a colleague emailed me from somewhere in the north of England to tell me that something interesting was appearing at that moment on the US television channel C-Span. I thought it strange that he would know that, as to my knowledge the cable and satellite television providers here in Britain don't offer access to C-Span. So I asked him how we was getting it.

Well the punchline to the story should be pretty obvious—"hello Mr. Internet Expert, it's on the *Internet*". I should have seen that one coming.

I had never thought to check C-Span's website. I can blame this on the fact that the internet television I remembered from a few years ago would deter anyone from ever going back. But thanks to C-Span's website with its streaming video, I was able to view the US presidential debates in 2004 at my convenience—not at 2:00 in the morning here in the UK—in full-screen mode, with excellent sound quality.

How hard would it be for social change organizations to do internet television? A bit harder than radio, for sure.

The bandwidth required to serve up continuous streams of video is considerably more than that needed for audio alone. Meaning that costs would be higher—both to the broadcaster and to the viewer (who really would need broadband access).

There have been examples over the last several years of activists using the net to make television programs available. A good example can be found in Vancouver, Canada with Working TV—a cable TV show produced with union support offering an alternative view of the world. (Its tagline reads: "From the point of view of those of us who do the work.")

Today Working TV is available not only to its regular Canadian viewing audience but to anyone with access to the net at http://www.workingtv.com. Working TV offers its content in Real, QuickTime and Windows media formats, and for those without high-bandwidth connections, they offer audio-only versions as well.

The Canadian Auto Workers union has been producing a weekly video broadcast for its website for several years.

To produce a simple television program for the web, all you'd need in addition to the software and hardware described above for doing Internet radio is a digital video camera. The very cheapest ones are cheap indeed, but to get good quality, a considerable investment may be required. Nevertheless, prices of digital video cameras are always coming down.

I don't think internet television is—to use an expression borrowed from television itself—ready for prime time. Not just yet. But when you take a look at what Working TV has on offer, you get a taste of what's coming next.

To sum up, can Internet radio help us change the world?

Yes, it can.

We on the left, we in the labor movement, who want to change the world—we must use every technology that makes our work easier and more efficient. We must adopt communications tools that allow to us to reach global audiences, to bring our message of social justice and peace to people who will never hear it from the traditional state-controlled or corporate-controlled media.

And that is the promise of Internet radio.

APPENDIX A

How to Listen

One of the obvious ways in which Internet radio differs from conventional radio is that in a book like this, you have to include a chapter about "how to listen". This is true of all aspects of the new communications technology and not only Internet radio. For example, if you want to make a telephone call over the Internet using what is known as Voice Over IP (VOIP), and if you've never done this before, you're going to have to be shown how. If you want to keep a digitized album of your family photos, you'll need to learn how to do it. That's the nature of the new technology—it is more difficult to use, and less intuitive, than the old technology. No one writes chapters in books about how to make a telephone call or create a photo album or listen to the radio.

The chapter is divided into two parts, hardware and software. Hardware is by far the simpler, so we begin there.

HARDWARE

Basically, if you have a computer or have access to a computer, and you're connected to the Internet, the hardware bit is already sorted out. Now we can move on to software.

Just kidding—it's actually slightly more complicated than that. The point is that if you have a relatively recent computer, chances are you have a sound card inside the computer. There are many different ways you can get a computer to make sounds, including an internal sound card, an external sound card, or even a sound card embedded in the computer's motherboard. It doesn't really matter how your computer does it, but if it can make any sound at all, you can listen to Internet radio.

Just because your computer makes sounds, it doesn't mean that sound is going to be particularly pleasant. I have a laptop with a terrible little speaker built in and the sound quality is absolutely awful. In the one of the places where I work, the computers have tiny speakers embedded in the bases of the monitors, with even worse sound. So while a sound card is absolutely essential, a decent set of speakers is also a very good idea.

A few years ago a friend who had just bought a new computer system invited me to help him set up something connected to the Internet. When I came into the room, I was greeted by the sounds of a powerful stereo system. I was amazed then to discover that I was hearing music playing out of his computer. He had purchased high-quality speakers and an amplifier/sub-woofer that made his little PC sound better than my stereo system. Later on, I bought a similar set of speakers to allow my son to enjoy the experience of PC gaming—though I later borrowed them myself to make listening to music on a PC all the more enjoyable.

Given a computer with a sound card, and a set of decent speakers, you're nearly ready to listen to Internet radio. The last bit of hardware which you need is a connection to the Internet.

There are basically two kinds of Internet connections these days which go by the technical names of "fast" and "slow". Slow connections are connections made using modems to conventional telephone lines. These are the connections, which peak at 56Kbps, that always begin with the screeching sounds you can also hear when a fax machine connects. There are even slower connections than 56Kbps—if, for example, you try to connect to the Internet using an ordinary mobile phone, your connection is closer to 9.6kbps. And of course there are still people with even older modems, running at 14.4 and 28.8Kbps.

Can you listen to Internet radio on a slow connection? The answer is—probably, but you won't enjoy it. Internet radio works best at high speed. So you should have, in addition to a computer with a sound card and speakers, a high speed connection to the net. If you're doing this at home, that will most likely be either an ADSL or cable modem connection.

For many if not most people reading this book, you already have all the hardware you need to listen to Internet radio. Yet my experience meeting people who have all the proper kit, but say that they "can't hear" radio on the net, has taught me that the complicated bit is the software you need.

SOFTWARE

Chances are, you use a PC running a version of Microsoft Windows. That's not necessarily what I'd recommend. I have Red Hat Linux installed on my desktop and I think there's a very strong case to be made the Linux is a more robust, stable and secure operating system than Microsoft Windows.

I also have friends who insist that until you've used an Apple Mac, you don't really know how much fun a computer can be. And they may be right.

But the reality is, more than 90% of you are using Windows in one form or another and that's what I'm going to focus on in this chapter.

If you have a recent version of Windows—for example, Windows XP—consider yourself lucky. You not only have one of the better operating systems that Microsoft has released, but you also have, built in to your operating system, software that allows you to listen to Internet radio.

Windows XP comes with a bit of software called "Windows Media Player". One of its features is a button marked "Radio".

Microsoft generously provides you with a list of radio stations you might want to listen to—a list which consists almost entirely of the same commercial stations owned by media monopolies that you could hear on your old FM radio. Why would you want to use the Internet for that?

Nevertheless, if you've got Windows XP (and possibly, earlier versions of Windows too), you've got the software you need to listen to Internet radio.

Unfortunately, it's not the best software for listening to Internet radio. The website of Live365.com, the largest Internet radio service, warns that if you use Windows Media Player "you may experience severe buffering delays."

It's also a Microsoft product, and there are many good reasons for progressives to avoid Microsoft products. Microsoft is an all-powerful monopoly which is intolerant of unions. Though most of us are locked into using Windows in its various incarnations as our operating system, we don't have to use the Microsoft products that come bundled with it. We can choose which browser we use to surf the Internet (and Mozilla Firefox and Opera are excellent alternatives to Internet Explorer), we can and should choose alternatives to the virus delivery system known as Outlook Express and use a real email client instead (Mozilla Thunderbird, Eudora, Opera, Pocomail, and Pegasus are good alternatives), and we can solve the problem of "severe buffering delays" by using one of the many alternatives to Windows Media Player when we want to hear Internet radio.

The use I use is the venerable Winamp, which I mentioned in an earlier chapter. It's very simple to use. If you have a new computer you probably don't have Winamp installed, but it's a very simple matter to download and install the latest version.

There are many other free software tools you can use to hear Internet radio. Live365.com specifically invites you try out RealPlayer, MusicMatch, Sonique, J. River Media Jukebox, and its own Player365 software. And those choices are in addition to Winamp and Windows Media Player.

In addition to all those, Apple has released—for the first time in its history—software that runs on Windows computers: iTunes. iTunes is a first-rate media player, great for playing MP3 files, Internet radio, and so on. But it also heavily promotes sales from Apples's iTunes online music service.

That's not unique to Apple. If you launch RealPlayer, you see ads for the various commercial partners who have allied themselves with RealNetworks. Windows Media Player promotes the sale of CDs that Microsoft would like you to buy. Player365 encourages you to buy a "premium" membership in the otherwise free Live365 site. There are ads everywhere, except when you pay for a service—and even then you sometimes see the ads. Winamp stands out as being ad-free, which is one reason why I like it. And probably one reason why AOL is now shutting them down.

Live365 radio stations are playable using all the software mentioned above, but this is not always the case with Internet radio stations. Live365 is so universal because it uses the MP3 file format, which is non-proprietary. Everyone who writes software for playing music on your computer builds in the capacity to play MP3s.

But if your radio station is being streamed as a RealPlayer file, from a Real Server, then the people listening are going to have to use RealPlayer client software. Many of the books and articles about Internet radio encourage you to have more than one bit of software on your computer because of these compatibility issues. In any event, if you have Windows XP, you already have Windows Media Player, so it's only a question of downloading and installing RealPlayer from the Real-Networks website (http://www.real.com).

So let's sum up. To listen to Internet radio, you need a computer that's connected to the net, has a sound card and speakers, and some kind of software that plays audio files. Chances are, if you have a computer you've bought in the last couple of years, you already have all this and you could have skipped this whole chapter.

APPENDIX B

How to Set Up Your Own Internet Radio Station

Setting up an Internet radio station is almost as easy as listening to one.

The problem is, whatever I tell you now is likely to be out of date by the time you read this.

When I first thought about setting up an Internet radio station in the fall of 2000, one of the options was Live365. They were offering a very basic package free of charge. That was no longer the case by the end of 2003, when I returned to site to set up Radio LabourStart.

A year from now, or five years from now, there will be different ways to set up an Internet radio station, with different costs. But certain basic things will go unchanged.

There are basically two things you need for an Internet radio station now or in the future.

The first is content. The second is a host (also known as a server).

Content refers to the audio files you will be making available for delivery over the Internet. These files can be in many different formats. A couple of years ago, I would have recommended that any Internet radio station you create be based on files that are played through various incarnations of RealPlayer—the pioneers of streaming multimedia. But today you have a very good option in streamed MP3 files instead, and there are some clear advantages in going this route.

It doesn't really matter whether your content will be in Real files, or MP3 files, or even QuickTime files. How do you create content?

This depends in large part on what it is you intend to broadcast. My own station broadcasts a mix of songs and talk, some originally produced and some taken off of recordings. This has meant that the creation of content involves, for us, a mix of different hardware and software.

The hardware is not very different from what I described earlier, when I told you what you needed in order to listen to Internet radio.

You will need a computer with a connection to the Internet—ideally a high-speed connection so that you can quickly and easily upload files to your server. (Indeed, a computer with a high speed connection to the net can itself serve as a host for your radio station, using SHOUTcast. But that's a bit more tricky to set up.)

The computer needs speakers and a sound card so that you can hear the content you have created. But in addition it needs two things that ordinary listeners to Internet radio do not need.

The first is a microphone. Some computers—like my laptop—come with a built-in microphone. But these are often not of the highest quality, so it worth your while to invest in a decent microphone.

I purchased a Sony microphone headset for the equivalent of $100 and am very pleased with it. Not long ago, I was interviewed by a journalist from the BBC who wanted to see the "studios" from which we broadcast our Internet radio station. She was surprised at the equipment we were using, having heard a very decent quality recording of my voice. I explained that given a quiet room and a decent microphone, you could get this kind of sound quality.

In addition to a microphone, which is something you'll have to buy, you will probably need a CD drive in your computer—which is almost certainly something you already have. You'll need this because chances are you'll use content (music, but not only music) which is available on CD.

An Internet-connected computer with sound card, speakers, microphone and CD drive—that's really all you need in terms of hardware to create content for an Internet radio station.

Then there's the question of software. Your PC does not come with built in software to make this task easy.

For example, Microsoft bundles with its computers a bit of software called "Sound Recorder". This seemed very useful to me at first—free of charge and allowed me to record from a microphone to any file format I wanted. Where's the catch? (With Microsoft, there's always a catch.) The catch is, your files can't be longer than one minute.

If you're a New Yorker like myself, no problem. I can speak very quickly. But for most people, the one minute limit makes Sound Recorder worse than useless. I wonder why Microsoft built that into the software. It's not like this is a demo version and if you pay them $29.95 you get the version without the limit. There is, as far as I know, only one version of Sound Recorder.

Microsoft in its Help pages for this software writes that "Using Sound Recorder, you can record, mix, play, and edit sounds." It doesn't say—anywhere—that you face this ridiculous 60-second limit.

Oddly enough, most independent descriptions this software don't bother to mention this extraordinary limitation either. For example, I have here a copy of "Windows XP Pro: The Missing Manual", published by the authoritative O'Reilly publishers. There are three full pages on Sound Recorder which tells you that the software "lets you capture the sounds of your world digitally" and "record various snippets of your life". Snippets indeed—the program is absolutely useless because of this limitation.

So the first bit of software you will need is something that allows you to record more than 60 seconds to a file. And ideally, it will record directly to the file type that you'll be using on your Internet radio station. As that file type is unlikely to be Microsoft's own WAV format (which is what Sound Recorder creates), that's another reason to use something else.

I use a program called Power MP3 Recorder (MP3 Sound Recorder) and it's available for download from http://www.cooolsoft.com. (That's not a typo; this company's software is so cool that they had to add another "o".)

There's a free trial version and a registered version that costs $19.95. There are other programs that do the same or similar functions.

Power MP3 Recorder has a number of useful features for anyone considering using it for creating MP3-based Internet radio shows. It records anything that passes through your computer's sound card, so you can use it to record from a microphone, or from a CD while it's playing, or from any other sound line connected to our computer, such as a cassette recorder, old-fashioned record player, radio or television. You have complete control over the bit rate which is important when creating content for Live365 stations (more on this later). But best of all, you're not dealing with Microsoft Sound Recorder's idiotic 60-second limit.

Even though Power MP3 Recorder can record CDs that are playing through your system, the more common way to convert music and other audio from a CD to a format that you can use on Internet radio is to extract or "rip" the music from the CD to your hard drive.

In this case, Microsoft Windows XP does actually come up with a solution. Windows Media Player will "rip" your CDs for you.

With these two bits of software—one an improvement upon Microsoft Sound Recorder, the other a CD "ripper"—you have all you need (almost) for your radio station.

I have found a use for just one more program and that's the open source tool known as "Audacity" (you have to love that name, right?)

Audacity is a free, cross-platform audio editor. It works on Windows, Linux and Mac and I've found it useful for one thing: combining audio from two different files. That's good if I want to add an introduction to a recorded song, for example. It's available from http://audacity.sourceforge.net

Attentive readers who have gotten this far and who are diligently trying out all the software I'm recommending may have by now noticed one disturbing fact. I keep on recommending programs for you to download and use, but there do always seem to be alternatives. Just a moment ago, I told you that Power MP3 Recorder could actually turn your music CD into MP3 files—so why use another program, Windows Media Player, for that purpose? And doesn't Audacity do the same thing that Power MP3 Recorder do?

The short answer is that there is a lot of overlap between these programs. Even the software I recommended earlier for playing Internet radio, such as Winamp or Apple's iTunes, can also be used to do things like rip CDs.

The point is to begin to assemble a toolkit, ideally made up of free tools, which does the job. Just like with a regular toolkit, you can use a wrench to bang a nail into a piece of wood, but a hammer is specifically designed for that purpose and will work better. It's the same with software.

The tools I've been describing so far are great for creating MP3 files which is what I've been using on my Internet radio station. There are other ways to do Internet radio and if you want to build your station based on, say, Real Player, you'll need to use different tools to create the audio files you need.

But the principle remains the same: you need software that can convert your voice coming through a microphone, or your music collection on CDs, into audio files that will be streamed by your server. To do this with streaming MP3 files using Live365's server, I've found the software described above to be very useful.

Which brings us to the second part of the discussion—the host or server.

There's a bit of a chicken-and-egg question here. The server you choose will help decide the file format you're going to use. For example, I had already picked Live365 as the hosting company for Radio LabourStart before I'd even thought about the file format I was going to use.

But once I had picked Live365, I had locked myself into using streaming MP3 files—and I don't regret this for a moment.

If you plan to use any of the alternatives I mentioned earlier in this book—such as SHOUTcast, A-Infos or Indymedia—you might also want to stick with the universally recognized MP3 format.

Alternately, you could decide that you want to go with the Real solution—meaning that your listeners would have to use RealPlayer to listen to your broadcasts. If you were to do that, you'd need to encode your files into the Real format, and host them on servers which are capable of delivering them. RealNetworks offers these solutions, as do other companies.

The same applies if you want to go for the Microsoft solution—you'd need to encode your files to Active Streaming Format (ASF) and your listeners would need to listen using Windows Media Player.

Apple's QuickTime format also has its own encoding software and if you want your listeners to hear your station, you'll need to encode to that format and they'll need to listen using QuickTime client software.

If you're willing to push the envelope, there's even a relatively new Open Source format for audio files which is gaining some popularity—but you'll have to get around the problem of its name. It's called Ogg Vorbis, and you might find this explanation helpful: "Vorbis is a completely open and free audio compression (codec) project from the Xiph.org Foundation. It is frequently used in conjunction with the Ogg container and is then called Ogg Vorbis." That's all clear now, right? In any event, a number of rather daring Internet radio stations are streaming their content using this format.

Because of the plethora of different file types, each one requiring different encoders, different servers and different clients, many websites now offer a choice of ways to hear audio content. It is quite common to give listeners a choice of Real or Windows, for example.

In any event, once you've made your choice, you have to make it clear to visitors to your radio station what software they need to listen to it—particularly if you're using a format (such as Real) which is not necessarily part of their Windows operating system. Usually, one includes the logos of the software so that first-time visitors can download RealPlayer or QuickTime or the MP3 player of their choice.

If you choose to follow what I think is the easiest route, which is using Live365, you should know what the different options are. The lowest-cost plan starts at $9.95 a month, and allows you store about 100 MB of recorded content. That allows up to 25 people to simultaneously listen to your station. It does not allow you to do live broadcasts.

Radio LabourStart is currently using a plan which costs $24.95 per month, and offers 300 MB of storage, up to 100 simultaneous listeners, and the option of doing live broadcasts with up to 30 simultaneous listeners. What does 100 MB of space mean in practice? For us it means about 350 songs, or more than 20 hours of content.

The most expensive off-the-shelf plan (and there are customized solutions as well) costs $44.95 per month and gives you 1,000 MB of space to store your audio files, and up to 100 simultaneous listeners in both recorded and live mode. That means you can have around 3,500 songs, or over 200 hours of content.

Some of the features you ought to know about in using a service like Live365 are its software, its message boards, and its statistics.

You'll almost certainly want to download and use Studio365. While there are other ways to upload music to your website and organize the music into playlists, Studio365 makes this easier. I found its most useful feature was the way it transformed any MP3 file into the exact format I had configured the site to play.

I should mention that when setting up your station on Live365, you have to decide in advance what quality MP3 files you'll be using. Big, high-quality files which will make your station sound like an FM stereo radio station will take up a lot of room on the server. I was restricted by the low-quality, mono files that WINS was distributing. The Studio365 software takes care of all this, and I don't bother to make any changes to any of the MP3 files I receive—it's all done while I upload them to the Live365 server.

Live365 attempts to build a sense of community among its broadcasters and its message boards are quite popular. These are grouped according to the type of music you broadcast. As much of Radio LabourStart's content consists of folk music, I've been visiting the Folk/Blues/Country board, using it both to post items about changes on our station and to read about what people with similar interests are up to. Nearly 800 messages have been posted to this board, so it is a pretty lively community.

One of the really nice features about using a service like Live365 is the statistics you'll be shown. These are calculated every day and once you've logged into the Live365 website you can view them. The "big number" to look at is what everyone in the Live365 community calls "TLH"—Total Listening Hours. This is the total number of hours your station was listened to. It is not the total number of listeners, which is a lot more difficult to calculate. Live365 tells you this number for the last month on your main page, and you can see daily breakdowns if you delve into the subject further.

If your total listening hours for a day is 24, that could be one person listening throughout the day, or 24 people each listening for an hour. When you click on "Stats Details" on the Live365 site, you get more of a breakdown. You can see how many streams were launched on a particular day, and this is a decent indication of the maximum number of listeners you might have had on that day. You can see the average time each stream was open, which is more or less the average time people stayed tuned to your station.

One interesting statistic is the number of "Station Presets". Many people when trying to listen to your station on Live365 will add it to their list of preset stations on the website. For Radio LabourStart after broadcasting for 10 months, that number was just under 500.

Finally, Live365 tells you where you stand compared to other stations—both overall, and within the main genre you've defined. For example, Radio LabourStart has sometimes come within the top 1,000 stations, but not often. Within our main genre (folk music) we are often in the top 20 stations. The reason why this matters is that some of your listeners will have found out about the station because they've visited Live365 and they've browsed or searched. The larger your number of Total Listening Hours, the higher you're going to appear in any list.

You can waste a lot of time studying your stats at Live365, just as people often waste a lot of time studying their website statistics (hits, page views, etc.). But this is a clear advantage over using some of the other, free services—because with Live365 you really do know how many people are listening. In fact, you can know in real time. Both the Studio 365 software and your account page on the

Live365 website will tell you how many people are listening at any given time. One of the enthusiasts in the Live365 community even wrote a bit of dedicated software to keep a little program running on your computer desktop telling you how many people were currently listening to your audio stream.

One last bit of advice for potential broadcasters: you really should have a website dedicated to your radio station. It's not enough to just have a link saying something like "click here to listen to our radio station" on your own site. You need to do a bit more.

We've created a dedicated website for Radio LabourStart on the main LabourStart website. It's gone through several versions by now, and the current version is based on blogging software to allow quick and easy updates. The website includes a link to play the station as well as a link to a page explaining how to play it, what software you need, and so on. But the core of the station's website tells listeners what's new, what's coming up, and involves them in the station. Listeners can send in feedback, request songs, and get involved. Musicians are invited to submit content, and readers are asked to join in the project. We also use the station's website to blow our own horn by publishing some of the fan mail we receive. You can even use the station's web page to solicit donations using an online payment system like PayPal.

Creating an online radio station is cheap and easy—and great fun. I hope you'll give it a try.

Glossary

ASF: Active Streaming Format. A Microsoft proprietary streaming file format for Windows Media Player.

Bandwidth: The capacity of an Internet connection, measured in bits per second.

Bit rate: In an audio file such as MP3, the bit rate is the number of bits transmitted per second; high bit rates mean high quality, but large, files.

Broadband: A transmission medium designed for high-speed data transfers over long distances. Cable modem services and ADSL are examples of broadband.

Buffer: An area of computer memory reserved for temporarily holding data before that data is used on the receiving computer. Buffering protects against the interruption of data flow.

Codec: Short for coder/decoder. A software program for converting between digital data and analog signals. Popular audio codecs include Real, Windows Media Player, QuickTime, Ogg Vorbis and MP3.

Compression: A process for removing redundant data from a digital media file or stream to reduce its size or the bandwidth used. MP3 is an example of an audio file that takes advantage of compression.

Connection speed: The maximum rate, in bits per second, at which data can be transferred between a network and a computer or device.

Download: To transfer a file over a network in response to a request from the device that receives the data.

File format: The structure or organization of data in a file. File format is usually indicated by the file name extension—such as MP3, ASF, WAV, RAM, or OGG in the case of audio files.

MP3: MPEG-1 Audio Layer 3. A digital audio compression algorithm that achieves a compression factor of about twelve while preserving sound quality.

Ogg Vorbis: An open source file format competing with MP3. Its proponents claim that it has higher fidelity than MP3.

Playlist: A sequence of audio files, such as songs. Radio stations both on the net and off use playlists.

QuickTime: Apple's software for streaming media (audio and video).

RealPlayer: The RealNetworks software used to receive video and streams in the Real format.

Rip: Extracting digital content, usually from CDs to a computer hard drive. Ripping usually involves conversion to a compressed format, such as MP3.

SHOUTcast: Nullsoft's internet streaming MP3 solution.

Stream: The process of transmitting digitized video or audio via the net, allowing end users to see or hear content in real time. See "buffer," above.

VDOLive: An early streaming video software.

WAV: Widely used uncompressed audio format. Usually more than 10X larger than MP3.

Webcast: The transmission of audio or video content via the world wide web.

Winamp: A popular player of MP3 and other audio formats.

Windows Media Player: Microsoft's software to viewing multimedia content on a computer.

0-595-34965-X